5

SECRETS

GREAT
DADS

KNOW

Books by

Paul Coughlin

FROM BETHANY HOUSE PUBLISHERS

Five Secrets Great Dads Know

Married . . . But Not Engaged (with Sandy Coughlin)

No More Christian Nice Girl (with Jennifer Degler)

No More Christian Nice Guy

No More Christian Nice Guy Study Guide

No More Jellyfish, Chickens, or Wimps

Unleashing Courageous Faith

PAUL COUGHLIN

5

SECRETS
GREAT
DADS
KNOW

BETHANY HOUSE
Minneapolis, Minnesota

Five Secrets Great Dads Know
Copyright © 2005, 2006, 2007, 2009, 2010
Paul Coughlin

Cover design by Lookout Design, Inc.

The material in this book is adapted from the following books by Paul Coughlin

> *Married . . . But Not Engaged*
> *No More Christian Nice Guy*
> *No More Christian Nice Guy Study Guide*
> *No More Jellyfish, Chickens, or Wimps*
> *Unleashing Courageous Faith*

Published by Bethany House Publishers
11400 Hampshire Avenue South
Bloomington, Minnesota 55438

Bethany House Publishers is a division of
Baker Publishing Group, Grand Rapids, Michigan

Printed in the United States of America

ISBN 978-0-7642-0768-6

CONTENTS

WE'RE DADS, NOT MOMS

There was a time when we made too much of the differences between men and women. And women usually suffered. Now our culture has worked double time to get us to believe there are no differences between the sexes. For example, some point to the fact that the DNA of men and women differs by only 1 to 2 percent. This doesn't sound like much, until you realize that this is the same percentage of difference between women and female chimpanzees. (My wife didn't feel particularly blessed when I enthusiastically shared this fact with her.)

Women and men differ physically, emotionally, and psychologically. Mothers possess a greater ability to understand infants and children; they are more able to "distinguish between a child's cry of hunger and a cry of pain."[1] Mothers release the polypeptide hormone *oxytocin* during pregnancy and breast-feeding, causing them to be more interested in bonding with children and engaging in nurturing behavior.

Fathers, by contrast, excel when it comes to discipline, play, and exhorting their children to embrace life's challenges. Physical play is far more important than most of us realize, promoting "social skills, intellectual development, and a sense of self-control."[2] A father's playful side teaches children how to regulate their feelings and behavior as they interact with others. Children who roughhouse with their fathers usually learn quickly that biting, kicking, and other such actions are not acceptable.

Fathers are more likely than mothers to encourage their children to take up difficult tasks, seek out fresh experiences, and endure pain and hardship without caving. "The bottom line is that fathers excel in teaching their children the virtues of fortitude, temperance, and prudence for life outside their family."[3]

I monitor what my kids are thinking, whether they need protection, in what ways they're struggling, how I can help them with their difficulties. It is not my nature to keep track of clothes the way my wife does, and I'm not about to add that one to my radar.

We're dads—not moms—so let's embrace this fact with gusto and the good kind of pride. We're not better than moms, just different, and this vital difference has been ignored and devalued to everyone's detriment. Men have felt dishonored and disposable. Women and children have felt abandoned in ways they may not be able to name but certainly feel in their day-to-day lives. Their lives have been missing vital nourishment for too long, like a body low on iron or vitamin B.

But change is afoot. Our value as men, as dads, is on the rise. Our essence is being called for again as in generations past, with a deep inner groaning. This call on behalf of society is real though still reluctant, like a father begrudgingly asking for directions on a family vacation. There's nobility to being a dad and that is coming back. Respect is mounting again like a wave a hundred yards or so offshore. We're coming to our senses. Handled with confidence and humility, we can erase much of the worry we have about the nature of a man and be a gift to those we are charged to honor, love, respect, protect, and guide.

I have children's best interests in mind. I've been a father for seventeen years, I've worked with children as a coach for more than ten, and I've written a book on parenting. I love kids, and I want them to fare well in the real world. I want them to fulfill their dreams and potential. I want them to walk hand in hand with God, to understand that nothing can separate them from his love. I want them to experience the strength of heart and clearness of mind that comes from genuine humility.

I want our daughters to know in the core of their soul that they are loved by God and valued by man. I want our sons to know in the core of their soul that they have what it takes to make it in life. I want our children to have the fortitude to persevere, the courage to create deep and abiding love (*agape*), and the will to undergo the difficult work that dirties the hands of fighters for peace and justice.

I want our children to be remarkable, better than average. Better at defending the small classmate who is pushed against lockers or ridiculed online. Better at befriending the one who is out of the clique or teased because she wears last year's shoe styles or a hairdo that is six months behind the fashion curve. Better at being less accepting of—and less silent about—what's really wrong and unacceptable in life. These children laugh more, play more, and weep more—they're emotionally attuned, spiritually vital, and pragmatically prepared to respond when virtue calls them to action.

Unfortunately, Christian and non-Christian parents alike are raising children who are passive, pleasant, and malleable rather than innovative, proactive, and bold. These "nice" children prevalently struggle with fear, anxiety, and loneliness, and later in life, relationship instability and divorce. Our goal as dads should be to create confident and truly virtuous kids who are capable of doing more than their part in obtaining an abundant life. These children become adults who lend their strength to others and help them obtain happiness as well.

How do we reach this goal? In the coming pages we'll look at the characteristics of great dads as well as some of the best things dads can do for their kids. I want to offer thoughtful, practical advice based on what I've learned, and it starts with the man you are.

GREAT DADS ARE GOOD GUYS

My name is Paul, and I'm a former Christian Nice Guy who finally realized that what we call valorous niceness is often cowardly passivity in disguise. Christian Nice Guys (CNGs) generally believe they should just let life happen to them. A large portion of the church tells them they should rarely if ever exert their will, and that possessing passion, boldness, and intensity is "worldly." *Those* qualities belong to "aggressive" and "proud" men (ironically, that would include the real Jesus who was mighty bold and intense when virtue called). Many have told me that it is far more Christian to live passively, deny your heart's desires, and keep your life in neutral because somehow this glorifies God.

As someone who was conditioned to always be pleasant, not to disturb others, and—for the wrong reasons—be quick to turn the other cheek, I held the classic distorted Nice Guy view of myself. I believed I was defective and bad not because of my sin, but because my perception was off. *Others* were worthy of respect if for no other reason than to have their human dignity affirmed. *Me?* Well, do what you want to me, because I—my thoughts, my feelings, my wants, my needs—don't really matter. *Other* people were normal; *I* was a sort of subspecies, a child of a lesser god.[1]

Why do I tell you this? Because Nice Guys aren't great dads. *Good Guys* can be great dads. Let me show you what I mean, because you might be a CNG too.

The church taught me to worry more about sin than purpose, more about keeping up appearances than searching for and embracing meaning. More about what I *shouldn't* do than what I *should* do. More about being defensive instead of offensive. More about being nice than being good. Fear of failure, of falling short, of not being perfect (even though we've tried) makes us paralyzed, immobile, and eventually indifferent.

Fear-based religiosity creates dangerous tension that

ruins marriages, careers, our children, and sometimes even our souls. We *should* avoid sin, for many reasons—that it separates us from God and from life is at the of top the list. *But the immobile life does that too; it's just harder to diagnose.*

Think about it, Nice Guys: Wouldn't it be great to view conflict as an event you could enter into with moderation, tact, and wisdom, the way you've seen other men embrace it? To be freed from the shackles of "niceness," a fearful vice that takes on the deceptive posture of virtue, an idol that distances you from God and from others? Marriages would be saved, our culture war would gain new and powerful members, children would have a dad to admire, missions would be launched, and God's redemptive plan would transform yet another dark realm of this messed-up world.

Nice can't confront this world's sources of pain. Niceness makes people agreeable, not good. Somehow we have mistaken niceness for righteousness.

Fred Rogers: Not a "Nice Guy"

Don't get me wrong. Gentleness *is* a virtue. I remember how warm I felt as a troubled kid, watching Mr. Rogers. He blessed me with his gentle ways, and he helped to settle my anxious, battered heart.

Fred Rogers was a *Good* Guy—a Nice Guy would never have worked so hard to love others. "Discipline was his very strong suit," said his wife, Joanne, after his death. "If I were asked for three words to describe him, I think those words would be *courage, love,* and *discipline*— perhaps in that very order."[2]

Nice Guys are weak in all three of these vital areas; they would buckle under the unfair jabs thrown his way. Fred Rogers was lampooned for his loving ways; he knew it and he continued anyway. Though he took great risks, they didn't show. He didn't *want* them to show, because he wanted to impart the gift of stability to children who lacked this critical nourishment.

He fought, through gentle means, against bigotry, injustice, and the devaluing of children during a shameful time in our history when children were to be "seen, not heard." Again, a Nice Guy wouldn't have (*nor* would he seek) the inner strength to undergo such labor: "He was able to find the courage and determination to use his knowledge and talents—and, in fact, his whole life—in the service of children."[3]

People who put down Fred Rogers reveal their own lack of perspective and understanding, for he was no fake Nice Guy—his love was real and pure. "Love isn't a state of perfect being," he reminded us. "It is an active noun, like *struggle*."[4]

Good Guy Masculinity Sees the World Clearly

There's an essential toughness that's intrinsic to real masculinity; part of this is in understanding how the world really operates since it's no virtue to be ignorant of such things. That goes to the heart of the CNG problem: Ignorance of the world's ways trips up our ability to have strength for what's right. The good news is you won't find this ignorance in the human pillars of our faith. Contrary to what you've heard, it's not a sin to embrace tough-minded shrewdness. In fact, it may be a sin if you don't.

For instance, in his gospel John records how Jesus did not entrust himself to the crowds that gathered around him: he was shrewd, and he kept himself separate. We can be sure that this upset people. Today, if you changed Jesus' name and told the story, we'd likely say that such a person was rude because he didn't follow commonly accepted principles of appropriate, thoughtful social engagement (much less meet the needs and desires of others). We've been taught to call such a person selfish. Christian men try to make everyone appreciate them, even though Jesus clearly didn't do this.

As for being shrewd, I can hear the chorus: *We're not supposed to know more about the world! We aren't supposed to be worldly!* But who's talking about being worldly? I'm talking about a Christian masculinity that understands how the world functions without buying into the world's destructive values.

True, God tells us we should have a child's heart, but many Christians, said C. S. Lewis, use this as an excuse to justify foolishness. Children exercise plenty of prudence, and God "wants us to be simple, single-minded, affectionate, and teachable, as good children are." He wants a "grown-up's head" that musters "every bit of intelligence we have to be alert at its job, and in first-class fighting trim.... He has room for people with very little sense, but He wants everyone to use what sense they have."[5]

We are to live with heavenly things in mind and with our feet firmly on the ground. We won't be redemptive voices for good if we don't grasp this. Personal piety alone won't cut it, but marry piety to shrewdness, as Jesus did, and you're on your way, Good Guy.

Our Children: Served Up Soft

I would be remiss if I didn't address the epidemic of raising children to be Christian Nice Guys and Girls, because we're rearing another generation to follow in our bland mediocrity. It's so much easier to raise healthy boys and girls than to repair shattered ones.

A compelling article in *Psychology Today* says we are a "Nation of Wimps" whose parents are going to "ludicrous lengths to take the lumps and bumps out of life for their children" (Nov/Dec 2004). Many young people are becoming Nice Guys and Girls right before our eyes—more responsive to the herd, too eager to fit in, less assertive in the classroom, unwilling to disagree with peers, afraid to question authority.

The sons and daughters of Christian Nice Guys have seen many more examples of living out the gentle virtues than the rugged ones, of witnessing what the innocence of doves looks like but not the wisdom of serpents. We have them isolated, immobile, and we're telling them to respect a subculture that in many ways doesn't deserve their respect. We're more concerned about providing them with coddled safety than we are about inspiring them to live as God desires. (I'll have more to say about this later in the book.)

Rabbi Shmuley Boteach says, "Your job as a parent is to ease that transition between the idyllic world of the sandbox and the cold world of adulthood as much as humanly possible."[6] This transition is *not* achieved through sequestered seclusion or bump-free living. Our kids need to see us venturing boldly into the tough side of life and handling conflict with wisdom and courage.

Special Care With Kids

Remember that rules without relationship lead to rebellion with kids. When confronting their behavior, leave them with the impression that you are doing so not because you have nothing better to do, but because you are concerned for their well-being. You are struggling to help them create a better life for themselves. Leave them with the solid understanding that you are in their corner. You have their back.

Weight of Life

Men tend to represent the weight of life to children, especially the clear, powerful and unbending boundaries. Father Time carries an hourglass—symbolizing time, the most unbending reality in our lives. Dads teach their children that they must adjust to time—it won't adjust to them. It is fathers more than mothers who are more likely to draw their children into confrontation with such boundaries. And Father Time clutches a sickle, which symbolizes more than death. It also represents cleaving, the creation of stark distinctions.

Sometimes, because of our aggressive tendencies (passive men have this tendency as well, but they may release it in overblown ways), we make this weight too heavy. If we aren't careful, what we intended to use to *instruct* becomes a medium through which we *destruct*.

Both our culture and our churches have told us that aggression is a bad trait. Men must strip it from their lives, we've been told, and the world suffers for this misguided message. Properly handled and focused, aggression is a positive and creative force (granted, *assertiveness* might be a better word, as *aggression* can have a needless and ego-centered combative connotation).

Just read the first few chapters of the gospel of John and you'll see that Jesus would not have completed his redemptive mission, fulfilling his Father's will in his life, if he had not been aggressive. Without this valuable trait, he would not have rearranged and even destroyed our many misconceptions about God. Aggression is a medium through which authority, backbone, and weight are delivered.

How can you represent this weight of life, to teach your children to focus, be aware, and change when necessary without crushing them?

We simply cannot be good fathers if we do not respect and harness *our* drives and instincts. Pretending they don't exist just confuses matters and sinks us further in the malaise of passivity, depression, and addiction.

How can you respect your aggressive tendencies (which for passive men often come out sideways and perverted) when you pretend they don't exist, and harness them for good? (While reading about the life of Jesus, see what he does with his aggressive behavior. Does he act this way for his own benefit, or is his purpose larger, grander?)

Children don't start off questioning our authority. They are usually filled with a natural grace toward fathers. But with time this can break down, especially when authority becomes abusive. Remember: Rules without relationship lead to rebellion. And when it does, Salman Rushdie's words pierce with painful accuracy: "The reality of a father is a weight few sons can bear."[7]

As fathers, we are charged to draw our children into confrontation with the reality of the world, but the challenge needs to be age appropriate and able to be completed, otherwise we run the risk of crushing—not growing—their spirit.

For example, my sons have moved approximately 60 yards of rock, soil, compost and bark dust into our backyard with two wheelbarrows. I hardly moved any of it. I taught them how to load a wheelbarrow toward the tongue and how to use your legs when loading a shovel. I told them that it's best not to do this kind of work during the middle of a hot summer day—a reality they ignored but then learned from. At first they complained like most teenagers. I waited for them to start singing Negro spirituals such as "We Shall Overcome." But eventually they got into the rhythm of life's realities and gave up the naïve and childish belief that these realities should bend toward them. Eventually they experienced the pleasure of a job well done. They took ownership of the project and pride in its completion. It was hard for them at first, and as dads are supposed to do, I didn't let them quit. I coached them through it.

If your relationship with your children has broken down, ask yourself: Have I laid down too many rules without the relationship required for those rules to be respected?

If so, work on rebuilding your relationship with your kids, not insisting on more rules. Show them you care—that you are in their corner.

Dads Are Essential to Their Children

The largest predictive factor in whether a child will graduate from high school, attend college, avoid crime, reject drugs, or become an unwed parent before eighteen is the presence of a father in the child's life. According to a recent Health and Human Services report, "Fathers play a unique role in fostering the well-being of their children, not only through providership, protection, and guidance, but also through the way they nurture the next generation."[8]

The same report makes it even clearer:

> Girls with active dads demonstrate heightened levels of mathematical competence, and boys with more nurturing fathers display higher levels of verbal acumen. It is worth noting, of course, that girls tend to struggle more with math and boys tend to struggle more with language. Having an active, emotionally invested father appears to help children overcome the intellectual weaknesses typically associated with their sex. . . .
>
> Fathers are more likely to foster independent, exploratory behavior on the part of their children, compared to mothers. . . . Children raised by engaged fathers are more comfortable exploring the world around them. . . . A playful, challenging, and nurturing approach to fatherhood is associated with more self-control and pro-social behavior among children through the course of their lives. . . .

Fathers help their children—especially their daughters—develop the self-control and the sense of self-worth that protects them from premature sexual intercourse and teenage pregnancy.[9]

FOR FURTHER THOUGHT

- What are specific ways you can build your relationship with your kids?

- What can you do to help your kids better understand you, which will help them understand who they really are?

- In what ways do your children need to be wise as serpents, and how can you help them obtain this insight?

- In what ways right now can you anticipate your children's difficulties, and what can you do to guide them through as opposed to saving them from life's necessary growth?

GREAT DADS
HAVE THUMOS

For years and years I was not connecting with or activating a special region within me, a dimension that my spiritual training didn't even address or, when it briefly touched on the matter, told me was off-limits or sinful. It's a God-designed area, within me and within you, where courage and its fruits—unsentimental love and a martial spirit (to name just two)—are forged and stored.

This is a soul region that the ancient Greeks studied, praised, and placed warning signs around. It's a place that is a gift to those we love—if we'll do the soul-work required to grow it and unleash it. It can also be a curse if it isn't sea-soned and disciplined. At times it appears elusive. It's a lost piece in our spiritual puzzle. For many of us, it's our absent ingredient, the missing link in our spiritual journey.

The Greeks called it *thumos* (sometimes spelled *thy-mos*). This powerful word bulges with meaning, and it doesn't translate into English without some hitches. God created men and women with thumos, a "fight drive," a courageous and animating spirit, without which we don't grow in spiritual breadth and depth, are unable to deeply love, consistently fail to lead or surmount the sins of our flesh.

Thumos, wrote the ancient Greeks, is one of three main parts of our soul, along with *logos* (head and logic) and *eros* (heart and emotions). It's found—or at least should be found—more in men than in women, mak-ing a man's spirituality and his earthly responsibilities similar but also different.[1]

It's Neither Heart Nor Mind

Your thumos is not a subset of your feelings or emo-tions. An awakened heart is invaluable for our spiritual life, but when overemphasized, it can actually lead us away from a rounded-out understanding of our God-created design. *Hearts alone do not lead us into worthy battle.* And hearts sometimes lead us astray.

Thumos is where our head and heart converge, quarrel, and then put feet beneath our courageous intentions. This is an integral part of our fulfilling the good works that God has prepared for us in advance[2]—if we have the guts (a blue-collar definition of thumos) to play our part by being obedient to transcendent causes larger than our own ego and appetites.

Just as our heart alone isn't adequate to enliven our spiritual growth, reason (thoughts, mind) provides clarity but doesn't provide strength and impetus. Our lives are only strong, purposeful, and meaningful when we *do something* loving, beautiful, freedom-giving, redemptive, and worthy of respect.

Those who have been shot at in the line of military duty will tell you that if they'd waited for courage to flow before they responded, it would have been far wiser just to have stayed in bed. Something else within them, from another region of their soul, kicks into action. Rarely does one feel courageous in the face of opposition, and so over-reliance on one's heart or mind can be a trap. Courage must be manufactured within that inner place where our inner heat is stored. No wonder what we call a Thermos is derived from the word *thumos.* Yet thumos-courage is not only part of the physical life, it can also have a moral dimension.

Thumos (Greek): Courageous faith. *Guts* (a blue-collar definition). A vital capacity for life: an expression, a movement, an action, and living that's right here and right now. A container of spiritual heat and spiritual juice. A pugnacious yet playful drive; an attribute that separates the men from the males.

All of us men must lay claim to thumos so that God's grace in us can construct a new and dynamic person. Most of us will never fight a physical battle against an enemy; we will use our thumos, or not, for moral courage against both the evil spirit of the age that erodes human dignity and also against our own tendency to take the easy way through life, which halts spiritual growth. We must harness thumos to rise above the mediocre, trivial, social-club Christianity in which we too often find ourselves, shaking off the fearful and uninformed critics who worship comfort instead of truth.

We have flexed compassion the world over to combat poverty and disease. But one of the most underreported reasons people's lives are so desperate isn't that they don't have the ability to feed and educate themselves—it's that others oppress them, rob them, maim them, and enslave them. Many don't need more bags of rice—not ultimately. They, like the estimated 27 million people in actual slavery, like the 160,000 kids who stay home *daily* from American schools for fear of being bullied, need justice to rain down upon them from the hands of righteous people who will fight on their behalf.

Courage—the ability to confront fear, pain, danger, uncertainty, or intimidation, whether for ourselves or for others—always includes some form of *sacrifice,* though today we use that word glibly, employing it to describe almost any discomfort.

You have sensed your redemptive thumos bristle in

the presence of wickedness and evil even though you felt fear and were tempted toward cowardice instead. Next time, don't pretend this conflict isn't happening. Don't fool yourself into thinking that you aren't irritated, that you aren't indignant (which means in part "much to grieve"), or that there isn't a battlefield right in front of your very nose. Honor those moments. And don't avoid them. Reason and emotion alone cannot deliver decisive action. It is through thumos that we marshal ourselves to join the battle, take charge of our family, and change the world.

Staying Power

Thumos brings wholeness to a man's fractured soul in many ways. Atop this list of healing is that it creates greater staying power, the absence of which is a source of great pain and shame for some men. Another term for "staying power" is *fortitude,* the ability to stick to a task and not give up. From this seat of animation flow both strength and endurance to fulfill difficult responsibilities, including being there for your kids day after day, year after year, especially when it is neither easy nor convenient.

In order for our thumos to grow, and with this growth help to heal our own souls and love others better, we need to sink our teeth into a juicier and grittier faith. This is one of the reasons why we created The

Protectors, the faith-based solution to adolescent bullying. Historically it has been people of faith who defend human dignity. Through The Protectors, men as well as women are able to work on behalf of justice, which requires more from us than when we create compassion, important as it is.

Another prominent way that noble thumos heals a man's soul is by reminding him that life is not about him. It drives a man to stubbornly connect his life to transcendent causes, to go out into the real world and redeem real-world problems, filling his life with the peace that only comes from consistently living out deep meaning and abiding purpose. We must get beyond "blessed assurance" as Christians and fight to do our part for the kingdom of heaven, alleviating suffering, protecting the weak, and creating justice and freedom.

Without thumos, a man cannot truly love. Extinguish this fiery core, taint it, or dumb it down, and you undo the dad and the good he might have done. Thumos at its best helps fathers love in the way they were designed to love: unsentimental, confrontational, sacrificial, practical, playful, powerful, prophetic, kinetic, unpredictable, and noble.

Our homes, our churches, and our nation need men with more than active hearts and keen minds. We need men with active thumos courage, and we need our culture to respect it and discipline it—not kill it. We face a battle to awaken it. The health of our souls depends upon this conflict being resolved effectively instead of conveniently.

Those in whom the Spirit reigns are gentle when gentleness is required, and they are bold with the life-giving Word of God, sharper in truth and wisdom than any two-edged sword,[3] when that's required. Here there is no contradiction but rather completion. Men, we need to possess tender hearts, tough minds, and a heated thumos in order to play our part in God's plan for our lives.

Courageous people who helped to rescue Jews from the Nazis shared three major characteristics: (1) an adventurous spirit that was both humane and purposeful; (2) identification with a morally strong parent or morally strong heroic figure; and (3) an ability to identify with socially marginal people, which involved a willingness to break with tradition and withstand persecution while pursuing justice and truth.

Thumos in Action

I am very proud of my friend Bob Just, founder of Concerned Fathers Against Crime (C-FAC), which helps single men, fathers, and their sons patrol their neighborhoods with cell phones, flashlights, and a tangible concern for others. They don't carry guns, and they don't get out of their cars if they see something suspicious. They call the police and let them handle it.

Bob started C-FAC fourteen years ago, and he's worked hard to fine-tune his unique program, a movement really, in order to bring justice, mercy, and order to his community. One of my sons and I have been on patrol with C-FAC, driving up and down the streets of Grants Pass, Oregon. At first I was fearful of being a bridge person: standing in the gap between righteousness and lawlessness; but the men I went with gave me the courage to lean into this gap and eventually, surprisingly, enjoy it. That's what brotherhood was meant to do. I felt the martial spirit grow within me, and I found the experience exhilarating—I wanted more of this noble-thumos work.

Bob says, "The concept of a 'band of brothers' digs deep in our souls. Our hearts yearn for a team to join and a righteous fight to win. However, these days most men are loners out of necessity rather than choice. Mature men don't have many opportunities to be on a real team. We are busy with our family lives and our careers. Still, our warrior instinct knows battles are won the same way football games are won—with a self-sacrificial team effort. For victory to be achieved, we know we must all pull our weight.

"Unit cohesion is the force that finally defeats fear. As a C-FAC team bonds and actually becomes a 'band of brothers,' all those fears of being too busy melt away. The shared experience of protecting the community builds team morale, and soon the men actually like the challenge and look forward to 'the hunt.' . . . We come to see that the true mission is not one particular patrol night or other; the mission is men gathering together to protect their community, to minister to one another, and to demonstrate to younger men and boys what it means to be a community father."

FOR FURTHER THOUGHT

- Read Matthew 23:23–39, and consider the role thumos played in Jesus' denunciation of the Pharisees. In what situations do you feel it would be right for a Christian to emulate Jesus' dealings with the Pharisees?

- One way to build courage is to be around people of courage. Name three people you consider to be courageous. Also name a courageous person (or two) with whom you could spend more time.

- In the sporting world, offense creates and defense destroys. Which approach better describes the way you have been living your life? What role has courage been playing, or not playing, in your decisions and actions, particularly with your children?

- Think about a time in your life as a dad when you showed thumotic courage. How did it make you feel? How do you think it affected your children?

SECRET #3:

GREAT DADS LOVE AND PROTECT THEIR KIDS

I lacked needed guidance as a boy. I set my own curfews and prepared my own (not exactly balanced) meals. Whether I did homework or not was up to me. No one checked. No one asked questions. I went to parties on weekdays in junior high and high school. It didn't matter. I didn't think that *I* mattered.

I know what it's like to feel condemned to live another day, to not *want* to live another day, but feel you must because you wake up and find that fate still has you breathing. I took stupid risks with my body, which made sense because I didn't affirm its value. And all the while I gave the world that Nice Guy smile.

Abandonment deals a young boy's heart one of the deepest wounds imaginable; he will most likely come to believe he is unworthy to receive love and affection.

Fundamental episodes of my childhood were a confusing mixture of conditional acceptance and profound abuse. My mother hit, slapped, battered, and humiliated me more times than I can remember. She was indignant if I dared to defend myself, so I learned to relax, to roll with the blows much like a stunt man. That way the beatings were shorter; more intense, but shorter.

Dad was a house painter who often worked seven days a week for weeks on end. He provided well, was very loving, but we needed him to provide more protection at home. My parents were first-generation immigrants to America, so there was no extended family for me to run to. There was no neighbor who showed a rescuing nature.

My father was often neutral during key periods of my youth. I wish he would have inserted himself more into my life, pursued me more. In the last year of his life, however, he gave me a gift I didn't know I wanted and to some degree didn't know I needed in order to live a less-encumbered, more purposeful life. He told me he thought I had what it takes to make it in life, a sentiment he'd never before shared in words. His blessing came a little late—after a mortgage, a wife, three kids, and the toll of typical adult struggles—but hey, it came! More important, he told me *and* showed me that he was in my corner. He cheered me on. My spirit soared to heights I didn't think possible, and I've been freer since that unexpected blessing.

It's vital that we fathers do the same with our sons, and also with our daughters. I emphasize boys here because emotionally disturbed boys outnumber girls four to one. I've seen it: Boys feel alone out there. When the essential question *Do I have what it takes?* is not affirmed by another man, guys are left to wonder and to wander. Though they may appear confident, many men question their own ability to provide for and protect a family, even to the point of ulcers or hypertension.

I know that some children will never receive such a blessing from their father. I almost didn't.

Men, I ask: *Do your kids know that they matter to you, that you love them?*

Dads Protect the Weak

Recently one of my boys didn't make a sports team. The news was delivered to him bluntly, deeply injuring his spirit. I've been in his shoes so I was familiar with the litany of words to come, the same ones I spewed like a lawyer more than twenty years ago when I didn't make an important team. He couldn't understand why he didn't make it when a handful of less-talented kids did. The world was no longer as it appeared; injustice had slapped him, and the realization spun his mind into anger.

I tried to comfort him. He allowed some hugs; refused others. He laughed, but cried more. He'd hit a wall. He said the following statements within ten seconds of each other, I kid you not: "It doesn't matter, Dad, it really doesn't. . . . They're idiots! They made a mistake!" His mind was reeling and his words didn't make much sense.

I tried to console him again. I repeated a familiar story, how I didn't make the varsity soccer team as a sophomore, and I knew I had better skills than most of those who weren't cut. That was true, but there was another truth I didn't want to admit: I was smaller than most as well. Varsity ball would have crushed me. Fuming and embarrassed, I set out to prove the world wrong. I was captain of the junior varsity team. I knew more about the game than our coach. Regularly I practiced on my own, working on the weak side of my game. I was a varsity captain the next year. I set a school record. He knows the story. He's heard it before. It helped, but not so much this time.

He wanted to go out with his mother to do some shopping. I told him it wasn't a good idea for him to go out with Mom on that pivotal night; that it would be wise to stay home. Home is a good place to be when you're in pain. He said I was wrong—then in the same breath, said yes; yes, I was right. Then he broke down, cried some more, and ran to his room.

My heart broke for my boy. He asked me to contact his coach to find out why he didn't make the team. He didn't have to ask me twice. I had his back. I wanted to know too.

I once worked with a man who had repaired planes on an aircraft carrier. He spent most of his time repairing leaky hydraulic systems and was sometimes forced to ground "birds" against the will of their pilots. He said he had no choice—it was his job to hold on to the planes until they were ready to fly again.

I look at parenting through similar eyes. It's my job to help my kids fly well, and occasionally this means keeping them away from the world for a spell, usually one long and mercurial night. There's time to be a homebody and seek refuge in a board game or a TV show. Home is a place to salve our miseries, to lay low while pain, a powerful and hated minister, searches for ways to get at us. When it comes to kids, timing is everything, so sometimes we need to tell the pain: *Not tonight. You can mold him tomorrow, but tonight he's mine.* Our kids need time to regroup and to handle life's necessary suffering with strength they wouldn't have otherwise—and they can, thanks to this spectacular creation called home, where masculine (Dad's) energy should be free to pulse and protect.

Telling our children's angry disappointments to get lost for the night is like applying the Lamb's blood to our doorposts; our children will know that God's mercies are new every morning, and that we're fully on their side too.

Use Words That Protect and Affirm

Words of affirmation like *strong, brave, talented,* and *valuable* are indescribably important for our children. These words, especially when combined with words that protect, say that you are completely behind your kids. Learn to back up your words with actions and your children will believe what they're told.

My father wasn't always passive. He did speak up and act; I just wished he'd done more of it during key times at home in my young life. I recall one vacation where I was allowed to get dirty from head to toe. All day long! Covered in hallowed mud!

I remember walking back to our trailer alongside my dad when a woman nearby offered her two cents: "If that was my son," she said in a voice like a sick crow, "I'd tan his fanny!" I didn't know what a fanny was—I had to ask my dad—but I knew I didn't want any part of my body tanned by her.

"Well, isn't he lucky he's not your son?" Dad said in his lyrical Irish accent with perfect comedic timing. He wasn't prone to such direct talk, so I feasted on every syllable. I stared at that woman with the smuggest look I could muster: *Well, looky here! See who I have in my corner?*

He told me, "There's nothing wrong with you, Paul. But there's something wrong with her." All wisdom began and ended with my father on that warm and muddy evening, and I couldn't have been more proud. Or secure. In this scary world that loves to prey on little children, I had a lion behind me.

We're Raising Our Own Biographers

Just to be clear, I've either committed all the parental sins I address or I've thought about committing them. This book isn't about blame. It's about reform and turning away from beliefs, practices, and trends that hurt our kids and our culture.

We all make mistakes, partly because going into parenting at first means going into it somewhat blind. Most of us get, or at least feel, sucker-punched now and again. In spite of the mistakes we make, we need to stay involved, love our kids, and let them know we're behind them.

We raise our own biographers, make no mistake

about it. They may not write books about us that will be read by millions, but they will say things about us that will be heard by others.

What do you want your children to say about you?

What do you think they will say about you?

Do the lists line up?

If not, what can you do today to change that?

FOR FURTHER THOUGHT

- When a parent verbally demeans or attacks a child, it's not about the child. It's about the parent's inability to parent, usually due to some trouble they brought from their own childhood into adult life. What troubles were you affected by? How does this shed light on the ways you parent your children?

- I listed one example of my father's protective words on my behalf. His words filled me with a sense of comfort and value. Now it's your turn. Do you have similar words coming from either your father or mother that helped you realize they were in your corner? Try to remember how good it felt and how much larger and freer you were able to live.

- What words can you use to bolster your children today?

SECRET #4:

GREAT DADS
GIVE THEIR KIDS
WINGS

Ominous research tells us that today's kids are more timid, risk-averse, and anxiety-ridden than past generations. Fear, my fellow dads, is our newest baby-sitter, our most prominent child-care consultant. The reasons are many, but one of the most misunderstood and under-reported is our nation's most pervasive preoccupation: overprotective parenting.

We coaches call them "helicopter parents" because

they constantly hover, and they know how to attack. Most have no idea how their micromanaging hurts their kids behind the scenes, in the locker room, on the bench. By taking everything into their own hands and trying to make life smooth and painless, parents prevent children from developing the abilities they need to actualize their potential.

I want to encourage you toward charting a better course for your children. When we're all racing in place on the same Tour de Fear hamster wheel, everybody loses—children *and* parents.

We're afraid that our children will fall behind their peers. We're worried our kids might not do as well as other kids. We're terrified that we'll fail, and that our children will grow up to be the everlasting proof of our inadequacy. Letting them learn and make choices and take calculated risks *feels* wrong, even broken somehow.

By living out of our fears, we've made parental panic culturally acceptable. But the apostle John, in proclaiming the truth of Jesus, made clear that where love reigns fear is thwarted (see 1 John 4:16–18). Instead of building entire lives and families on a foundation of fear and frenzy, we can choose to equip and empower our sons and daughters for a future of fullness.

Ultimately, kids need to learn how to fly, and we must ask: Just how strong can their wings get if they're never allowed to use them?

We run to find quick answers and complete solutions to any little problem our children face. We do this whenever we have little or no faith that the issue could be worked out over time and doesn't need constant attention and intervention. We speed down to our child's school and bring them their homework assignments and books because they carelessly left them at home, instead of letting reality sink in, teach, and minister. We don't allow kids to play even on safe streets because we're freaked out about kidnapping. Many men, like me, not just mothers, struggle with parenting that smothers.

Contrary to our assumptions, kids who receive constant parental protection don't do better in life. When they're too often harbored from inevitable hardships and challenges, they do not develop a keen understanding of their own abilities and weaknesses. Sometimes they become overconfident, processing a distorted sense of themselves. They behave as if they are the center of the universe because, well, they have been for years. They are self-consumed and make others suffer from their excessive self-esteem, a common denominator for bullies. If you want to know why some children today are so thoughtless toward others, look no further than their over-parenting parents.

But most of the time they lack confidence, some to the brink of social anxiety and clinical depression, making them prime targets for childhood bullying that can persist into adulthood.

It is a common mistake to hold on to the things we love too tightly. It can feel so noble and so right. But good intentions aside, the consequences of wrongly raising our kids can be deadly.

Kids Need to Be Allowed to Feel Bad Sometimes

While speaking to parents about raising kids with successful character, Dr. Henry Cloud was asked:

"If there's one thing that's most important to teach children about success, what would it be?"

"I would teach them how to lose," he said.

A woman tilted her head, looked at him strangely, and asked, "Why in the world would you want to teach them how to lose?"

"*Because they will,*" Cloud said emphatically.[1]

The most important lesson children gain from losing is that *the difference between winners and losers is not that winners never lose.*

The difference is that winners lose well, and losers lose poorly. As a result, winners lose less in the future and do not lose the same way that they lost last time, because they have learned from the loss and do not repeat the pattern. But losers do not learn from what they did and *tend to carry that loss or pattern forward into the next venture, or relationship, and repeat the same way of losing.*[2]

This fundamental building block of successful living is being denied a growing number of our children. In various ways, their parents are not allowing them to fail in a constructive way because they fail to distinguish between an experience that is *hurtful* and one that is *harmful*. An experience that is hurtful causes pain but not damage. Harmful experiences cause both pain and damage. Pain is a dreaded minister, but we cannot deny that it does minister when handled with humility enough to learn from it and wisdom enough to transcend it in the future.

When Fear Drives Our Lives

Most overprotective parents don't use clean intuition; the real problem, frequently, is that they think they're using it. But true intuition leads to good results. Overarching fear, the driving force of worry, doesn't, even when it's couched in ways that in the short term appear good and noble to other overprotective parents. *When we're convinced that life is a tragedy waiting to happen, our kids suffer.*

I remember when what I called intuition backfired. I'd hired three men to move my hot tub, and when they pulled up and jumped out of their truck, they looked to me like they had just been released from prison. My daughter, uncharacteristically, went to open the door.

My blood pressure soared. A primal sap flowed from my gut throughout my body. I yelled, "Don't open the door!" and she escaped to her room.

I helped them move the tub, a beast of a job involving nearly six hours of difficult labor. I don't claim to have gotten to know them. I enjoyed working alongside them, and while I made sure they didn't enter my home, none of them gave me the willies.

What flared up inside me when they arrived wasn't intuition. It was an inclination via stereotypes that set off all kinds of warning bells in my head and I sounded the alarm loud and clear. Not to say I shouldn't have had any thought to safeguard my family. But knowing what I know now about which kids are abused and by whom (90 percent of sexual abuse is done by someone the child knows, not a stranger), I would be more productive observing relatives at family functions than worrying about hot-tub movers!

Ask your friends if they think you're overprotective of your children. Ask a certain kind of friend, someone you know will be truthful, even if it means he makes you uncomfortable at times. Ask someone whose perception you admire and who isn't prone to gossip or harsh criticism. Tell him he's free to tell you the truth, even if it hurts, and that you won't hold it against him afterward. Then truly listen and don't correct. Do not deny his claim. Instead, ask for clarification and if possible, examples. Mourn your mistakes if you need to, then act on the information you've been given. This is how great dads fine-tune their intuition.

In order to find the line between protection and overprotection, we need to take an honest look at our own understanding of who we are and how we relate to others. Specifically, we need to discover if we are too passive or too aggressive with others; one way or the other, our children are likely to inherit or incorporate much of what we display. If we show them an assertive approach toward life, they will be leagues ahead in knowing how to ward off anyone who would take advantage of them.

Passive people either react to life's issues, or underact instead of being proactive; they may or may not respond, but either way they do not initiate. Aggressive people overreact to what's happening around them. The passive and the aggressive alike are usually motivated by fear.

Assertive dads are proactive, which helps them create the right boundaries for themselves and for those in their charge. They respond with the right amount of power *and* grace. They don't hurt people unnecessarily, but they do get their point across. They know that it is unwise to use a hammer in a relationship when a screwdriver is needed. They have an air about them that acts as a repellant to would-be abusers.

Assertive people build good fences between themselves and others, and though they're no one's fool, they are not cold, distant, or cut off from others. Their personality opens many gates, but only to the right kind of people. They're comfortable in their own skin. They don't feel the need to control others, and they're not controlled *by* others. Most everyone, except the abuser, likes the assertive person. They're not mastered by fear, anxiety, or worry and so their perception of life and their intuition are both clearer than average. That's where we want to be as dads.

FOR FURTHER THOUGHT

- What did your trusted friends tell you about your parenting? Are you overprotective? If so, with the same friends, talk about ways you can develop your children's wings. (You might start by reading my book *No More Jellyfish, Chickens, or Wimps,* in which the topics of this and the next chapter are more fully developed.)

- It's time to become more assertive. The aggressive, who are motivated by unrecognized fear, overprotect and their borders become impenetrable—they tend to lock their children away from the world. It might be time to start including gates in your fences so that when your children move into life on their own, they will be neither painfully awkward nor wildly inappropriate, and most important, they will be a non-target for predators. What gate or gates can you create for your children?

GREAT DADS RAISE CONFIDENT, ADVENTUROUS KIDS

Our goal should be to create confident, adventurous, and truly virtuous kids who are capable of doing more than their part in obtaining an abundant life. These children become adults who lend their strength to others and help them obtain happiness as well.

What has happened to make parents discount the more muscular virtues such as courage and integrity?

These are obtained, sculpted, and bolstered by far more than requiring the standard "Yes ma'am," "Yes sir," and "Thank you"—and much more than memorizing verses or reciting prayers.

Courage, also known as fortitude, is the ability to confront fear, pain, danger, uncertainty, or intimidation, whether for ourselves or for others. Courage, one of the four "cardinal virtues" (along with wisdom, temperance, and justice) is pivotal, because in order to truly possess any virtue, a person must be able to sustain it in the face of difficulty. Courage is the foundational virtue upon which all others rest.

Yet how often do we diagnose a behavior as cowardice? For instance, what do you say when your son tells you about a bullying he witnessed but didn't intervene—just stood on the sidelines with the group? Have you helped him figure out that the sludge-like feeling gumming up his soul is a result of cowardice? Do you explain that cowardice is a normal but insufficient response to seeing someone unjustly treated or cruelly humiliated? Do you teach him that being wise and acting thoughtfully does *not* mean he is also to remain frozen, inert, and innocuous? Do you tell him it's a sin, right up there with lying (Revelation 21:8)?

Many parents have never even had a conversation with their children about cowardice. Warning against its corrosive nature isn't usually on our parental radar. Instead, most of us are quick to warn our kids to avoid getting too involved (or involved at all) when someone is mistreated because of the collateral damage it may do to them. *This is in direct defiance of how Jesus told us to live* (see Luke 10, the parable of the Good Samaritan). And we're overlooking the far-reaching damage of cowardice itself: Ultimately, cowardice can be as destructive as drug addiction.

Kids need to see at least one parent living courage, which is far more caught than taught.

Courage, Honor, and Dignity

Some argue that fear, not hatred or apathy, is the exact opposite of love. No matter the technicalities, we need to let our children know that while fear *is* a major enemy of love, it's always present when we're given the opportunity to grow courage or cowardice.

To give courage a chance to grow, we need to expose our children to the concept of honor, which is concerned with more than one's own dignity, important as that is. Honor is connected to other virtues, such as justice, loyalty, and fidelity. Honor values others and truth so much that it motivates a person to protect their value and worth. Honor, properly applied, says John McCain, is "concerned with the rights of others."[1]

In order for kids to embrace honor, we need to help them cultivate dignity. This doesn't mean we encourage them to fight every force that threatens their dignity.

It does mean they recognize that when their value is or has been under attack, sometimes wisdom dictates overlooking the offense, and sometimes wisdom signals responding in defense. My children know that when they have conflict with other kids, they need to allow their opponent to retain his dignity. Not only does this often turn away an assailant's wrath, it tends to keep children from making unnecessarily long-term foes.

Additionally, we must help our children understand the distinction between outrage and anger, a distinction I've often missed. Anger might stimulate impetuous courage, but of all degrees of courage this is the least effective. *Outrage,* in this context, means to take moral offense at something. Outrage is tied closely to our understanding of *indignation.* To possess righteous indignation, our children need to see us grieve the pain and suffering of others. Then people's trials and troubles begin to take actual shape and form for our kids, and this helps other people appear on their psychological radar screen as they build thoughtfulness, compassion, empathy, love, and courage in their hearts and minds.

This kind of growth takes practice, and it requires the freedom to make mistakes as they grow. Don't be too quick to point out that your son or daughter is getting "too upset" about something—listen to them, learn from them. If needed, lovingly point out when your child is failing to express indignation over unrighteousness and injustice. We want our children to become *more* passionate, not less, just like the real Jesus, who was more passionate than those around him!

My daughter, Abby, has my go-ahead to embrace the rugged virtues, which includes defending herself physically and emotionally. She's free and comfortable with her own power to act, and because of this, she's willing to sacrifice herself for others. (*That's* virtue.)

Just before I was to speak to Abby's first-grade class on writing, her teacher, Mrs. McCoy, asked the kids what they thought about Abby. One girl, the only student with a missing limb, spoke of admiration.

"She saved me. I think Abby"—she gave an adorable dramatic pause—"is a good person."

I later found out that Abby had fought for and rescued her one-armed classmate from two girls determined to beat her up. Abby got scratched on her face while defending a physically challenged person.

That little girl spoke those words about Abby with as much reverence as a believer talking about God. And, in a sense, she saw a side of God. She saw someone fight for justice and defend the weak, someone dear to God's heart. My daughter reflected God's nature.

The Spirit of Adventure

One of the best ways we can help our kids develop confidence and courage is to give them the spirit of adventure. One of our greatest advocates for cultivating and rediscovering this spirit of adventure is John Eldredge, who writes,

> Adventure is important for kids. It helps them test their mettle. But it needs to be the right kind of adventure. Adventure with a purpose, in the service of something larger than their own desire to pump adrenaline and other chemicals through their veins that give them a legal high and nothing more. Expensive self-indulgence.[2]

Helping Kids Experience Adventure

1. Get them into Scouts.
2. Sign them up for church groups that do real adventure.
3. Enroll them in sports, understanding the difference between recreational and competitive sports. If your child is not as skilled as his peers, the recreational level is usually the right choice. If he's skilled in a sport or is a quick learner and is motivated to get better, then the competitive level is a good choice.
4. Send them to summer camp (and do not call them).

I once inherited a soccer player whom a previous coach didn't want because he "didn't behave himself." He had a reputation for being a hothead. There was intelligence to his passion that sometimes spilled into anger, but he wasn't an angry kid off the field. He wanted to do well and was frustrated when he didn't. He didn't like people taking cheap shots at him, either. He wasn't a passive participant in sport or in life.

I like players who have what I call "the jalapeño factor" in them—another way to say they have a spirit of adventure or passion for life. Though I was warned about this kid, that he might cost me a game by getting a red card or committing a major foul in the penalty box, he never did so in three full years. He never lost us a game. Instead, his passion, which I helped to channel, has helped us win many a contest. His teammates even voted him captain.

It's a tragic day when adults feel the need to kill a child's heart and passion. There's a sinister element to it. I think many adults try to drive passion out of a child's heart because it's disruptive to our comfortable and highly scripted lives. There's unpredictability in the younger spirit that frightens us. It questions our assumptions and rationalizations. It refuses to conform, and we do love conformity. Their power isn't always offensive—rather, it strikes fear in us, which we find offensive.

Kids need help figuring out where to put such prancing energy, not how to kill it. They need help making it serve others and not just their own ambitions. It's a unique power that can help the timid and the weak.

Becoming Stronger

I love the boys I coach; it's not easy for me to see them get hurt. My heart is not made of stone—I know what it's like. I've been knocked out four times in my life—every one of them on a soccer field. Nevertheless, my head knows something that my heart needs to obey for the good of these young men. I do not repeat the sick athletic myth that pain equals weakness. Rather, I help my boys get stronger through the pain.

I'll have players, usually in the second half, who raise their hand for a sub. They aren't injured. They're tired. I can take them out, but there are times I'll shake my head and refuse, because I want them to learn something about themselves: They're able to endure more than they think. I have faith in their abilities and in their strength. *I know he has what it takes, even though he doubts himself. He needs to know all of this, but he won't until he works through it himself.*

Kids—girls as well as boys—sometimes need to experience the usual hardships of life. It's the only way they will find out that life's inevitable pain isn't going to kill them, that it can make them stronger. And it will, if we parents help them handle it properly.

FOR FURTHER THOUGHT

- "Your job as a parent is to ease that transition between the idyllic world of the sandbox and the cold world of adulthood as much as humanly possible," says Rabbi Shmuley Boteach.[3] What are you doing to ease that transition for your kids while instilling in them the courage and sense of adventure that will make them strong?

- Great dads exercise what I call their "kingly power," an ability to create clear and healthy boundaries by reaching beyond their families and working for good in their churches and communities. The Protectors (theprotectors.org) is a faith-based answer to adolescent bullying in public schools, private schools, Sunday school—wherever children gather. Through our *Courageous U Tour*, live school presentations in both private and public schools, we provide training and inspiration for the four major groups in what we call the "theater of bullying." We help targets, bystanders, bullies, and authorities to change their roles to defend human dignity and create schools that are safer, happier, and healthier.

DOMESTICITY

Dad, you have what it takes to raise and nurture your children—to be a great dad. Never forget that one of the greatest things you can do for your children—and your wife—is to nurture them within the arms of domestic life.

Domestication, which at its best is the demonstration of love, is good for men as long as we aren't required to live by a purely feminine understanding of it. We must make room for a melding of both feminine and masculine definitions of what it means to love and what love in a home looks like.

Male domestic love is often not demonstrated

through sentimental actions; Emerson Eggerichs points out that Jesus' loving actions rarely fell on the sentimental side. We guys are inclined to give physical and tangible acts of love.

For instance, I replaced a sewer line behind my house, a very unpleasant task, to say the least. Another time, with a freshly separated shoulder, I replaced a sump pump under our house, even though the pain was incredible.

I felt good after doing these projects and more. I endured discomfort for my family's betterment. It was my way of saying, "I love you guys."

We show love to those with whom we share our dreams as well as our pain—*communication connects us;* so guys, let's keep talking.

In this group that I call my own, usually during movie nights at home, I survey our darkened living room and take inventory of this small, five-person colony of mine. Limbs dangle from couches and overstuffed chairs. Someone's grousing for a back rub, scalp massage, or a glass of cold water. Someone throws out an observation about what just happened in the film, and the rest of us weigh it in our minds. Sometimes the responses I hear are funny and wise. Our kids are learning to make such comments *between* dramatic moments so they don't get *shush*ed.

I know this domestic scene will end. They will leave our home and usher in indelible changes. They will depart, if not in prosperity and opportunity, then in folly or (God forbid) tragedy. Nothing stays the same. There's no instant replay of these winsome moments; you have to savor them as they're fed to you because you can't reheat them. I sense that these rich moments, which grow and end at the same time, are the better portions of life.

During these times, when I'm at my best, I sacrifice a part of myself in the hope that some love will settle in, some hope and faith too. When my wife and three children need these gifts, they'll find them giving ballast to their lives much like the great hand of God.

These limbs lying leisurely along with mine are connected to my children, flesh of my flesh, destined to struggle with my judgments that are usually just but sometimes petty. When the natural blinders of youth fall from their eyes, they will see me for who I really was as a father.

My hope for myself is the same for you, my fellow dads: When our children reach the age of introspection and survey the grand canyon of their childhood, they will conclude in the smithy of their soul that their father was not some reality that few children can bear. Instead, we will be remembered, and later mourned, as kingly men of deep and abiding love, bolstered by courage, an eternal gift from which no experience can separate them or tear asunder.

Notes

INTRODUCTION
1. Brad Wilcox, speech in Qatar.
2. Ibid.
3. Ibid.

SECRET #1
1. My book *No More Christian Nice Guy* will give you a fuller understanding of the Nice Guy problem and ways to overcome it (Minneapolis: Bethany House, 2005).
2. Fred Rogers, *The World According to Mr. Rogers: Important Things to Remember* (New York: Hyperion, 2003), 7.
3. Ibid.
4. Ibid., 53.
5. *A Year with C. S. Lewis* (New York: HarperCollins, 2003), 283.
6. Rabbi Shmuley Boteach, *Face Your Fear: Living With Courage in an Age of Caution* (New York: St. Martin's Press, 2004).
7. Salman Rushdie, *The Moor's Last Sigh* (New York: Random House, 1995), 331.
8. Brad Wilcox, *The Importance of Fatherhood for the Healthy Development of Children,* Child Abuse and Neglect User Manual Series. (Washington, DC: U.S. Department of Health and Human Services, 2004).
9. Ibid.

SECRET #2
1. Thumos is a mighty gift, and like many gifts, can also be a burden. For more about thumos, read my book *Unleashing Courageous Faith* (Minneapolis: Bethany House, 2009).
2. See Ephesians 2:10.
3. See Hebrews 4:12.

SECRET #4
1. Dr. Henry Cloud, *Integrity* (New York: HarperCollins, 2006) 159.
2. Ibid., 160. Italics in original.

SECRET #5
1. John McCain and Marshall Salter, *Why Courage Matters: The Way to a Braver Life* (New York: Random, 2004), 206.
2. John Eldredge, *The Way of the Wild Heart: A Map for the Masculine Journey* (Nashville: Thomas Nelson, 2006), 97.
3. Boteach, *Face Your Fear.*